JN409881

The Day the Green Frog Counts the Marbles

Collection of Children's Poems for
Natural & Environmental Protection

Author : KWON, Daeja

Publisher : Bookland
#1108, Hwanghwa Building,
320, Gangnam-daero, Gangnam-gu, Seoul, Korea
Tel. 82-2-732-4574, 82-53-252-9114
Fax. 82-2-734-4574, 82-53-252-9334
http://www.bookland.co.kr
E-mail: bookland@hanmail.net

ISBN 89-7787-905-8 03810
ISBN 89-7787-906-5 05810(E-book)

Collection of Children's Poems for
Natural & Environmental Protection

The Day the Green Frog Counts the Marbles

by **KWON, Daeja**

Bookland

시인의 말

해와 달이 밝아서
어둠을 밝히듯
수증기가 구름 되어
눈, 비로 다시 오듯이
새싹 돋아 꽃 피고
바람에 향기 날아
벌, 나비 꿀 따고
잘 자란 열매들이
우리에게 힘을 주듯이

아름다운 자연 문화
소중하게 가꾸어가며
지구환경 보호하는
밝은 마음 배우는
어린이와 학생들이
나라의 희망이며
지구의 보배인 만큼
저의 소박한 마음을
정성을 다해
엮어 보았습니다.

지은이 *권대자*

Dedicating my Writings

As the sun and the moon light the world from the dark,
As the steam becomes clouds to return as snow and rain,
As buds grow to flowers,
As winds carry fragrances,
As bees and butterflies collect honey and
As the well-ripen fruits please us,
The nature is grateful and beautiful.

I dedicate my writings to the children and the students
who should learn how to take care and grow the beautiful nature
and how to grow better global environment.
Since they are our country's hope and world treasures,
I wrote this book for them with my best sincerity and love.

KWON, Daeja

PART 1

물소리와 꽃향기

The Flowing Water Sound and the Flower Fragrance

PART 2

빗방울은 예술

Raindrop is Art

PART 3

5월의 초록빛

Green in May

PART 4
청개구리 구슬 세는 날
The Day the Green Frog Counts the Marbles

PART 5

가을이 주는 선물
Present from Autumn

1부

물소리와 꽃향기

Part 1

The Flowing Water Sound And Flower Fragrance

물소리와 꽃향기

산골은 깊어서
계곡물이 졸졸졸
얼음 속에서 흘러도
그 편안한 소리는
자연의 자장가

팔공산 봉우리에
흰 눈이 녹지 않아도
노란 산수유꽃
매화꽃 향기는
자연의 숨결

The Flowing Water Sound and the Flower Fragrance

Trickling, trickling, trickling,
The sound of flowing water
Under ice in a brook
Is the sweet lullaby
Of the Mother of Nature.

Even though the head of Palgong Mountain
Is white with snow
The yellow corni flowers
And the fragrance of plum blossoms
Are the breath of nature.

2월에 핀 복수초

얼음 녹은 촉촉한
흙을 비집고 2월에
쏘옥 올라온 너

추울까 봐
따뜻한 햇빛이
아기처럼
포근히 안아주니

노란 웃음을
활짝 웃는구나
엄마 품의 아기처럼

Adonis in February

An adonis
Faces up
From melted ground
In February.

Not to be cold
The warm sunshine
Hugs it
As if an infant.

Yellow smile
On its face
Like a baby in mom's arms.

풀밭의 속삭임

무심히 지나다니던
풀밭에서
실바람 타고 들리는 소리

사람들이 밟고 다녀도
밤하늘 반짝이는
별 보고 꽃을 피웠지

그래 그래 나도 나도

튼튼한 뿌리가 있어
밤새 이슬 머금고
햇빛 받으며 쑥쑥 자랐지

그래 그래 나도 나도

비가 내려 더욱 풍족한
흙 무대에선
두려움이란 없지

그래 그래 나도 나도

풀밭 가족 오순도순
풀벌레 벌 나비 손님과
환희의 미소를 머금고
속삭이는 소리

Whispering from the Grass Field

It happened to me to hear
The voices in the breeze
From the grass field

Though being stepped down by people
They bloom flowers
Under the twinkling stars in night sky

Yes, yes, me, too, me, too.

Thanks to their strong roots,
With night dews
And the sun they grow bigger and bigger.

Yes, yes, me, too, me, too.

On earth stage
Being fertilized with rain
There is nothing to fear.

Yes, yes, me, too, me, too.

Happy grass family
Holding hands of bugs, bees and butterflies
Speak in whispers
With bright smiles.

학교 친구 내 짝꿍

처음 만난 친구
우리 반 내 짝꿍
나는 김복이야
나는 순이야 김순이
그래 반가워 나도
우리 친하게 지내자.

사이좋게 지내자
두 마음 마음이 모여
착한 어린이 되어
공부하면 재미있고
즐거워서 웃고 또 웃고
집에 갈 때, 내일 또 만나!

My School Seating Mate

I met her for the first time
As my seating mate
"I am Bok Kim, and you?"
"I am Suni, Suni Kim"
"Nice to meet you"
"Let's be good friends"

"Let's be nice to each other"
Two different minds became one.
Two good children
Study together with fun,
Laugh with happiness,
And say "see you tomorrow" when we go home.

어제와 내일

하루 종일
가랑비 내리던
어제는
책 읽기에
즐거웠다

뉴스에 내일은
날씨가 맑음
체육시간에
축구가
재미있겠다.

Yesterday and Tomorrow

Yesterday
It rained
All day long.
It was good
For book reading.

Tomorrow the news says
Will be clear.
In our P.E. class
We'll play soccer.
It must be fun.

백합 향기 좋았다

백합이 활짝 웃는 날
바람 타고 솔솔솔
창문으로 들어와서
집안 가득 백합 향기

엄마 누나
화장품 향기보다
나는 좋았다
백합 향기가.

Fragrance of Lilies was Good

On a day lilies smile happily
Their fragrance visited through
Windows by wind.
My house was full of lily fragrance.

I like the lily's fragrance
Better than cosmetic smells
Of my mom and sister.

독서는 즐거워

책 속에서 만난 친구
운동도 열심히
공부도 열심히 하면
성공하는 길이 있어
좋아-.

선생님 말씀도 있고
생활의 지혜도 있고
책 속에 착한 친구도 있어
독서는 즐거워
나는-.

Book Reading is Fun

My friend I met in a book
Exercised hard,
Studied hard
And finally succeeded. “Good”

There are my teacher’s words,
Wisdom of life
And good friends there.
Book reading is fun.

흰 장미 향기

꽃밭에 흰 장미가
곱고 고와서
바람이 놀러오고
해님도 놀러오고

흰 장미 꽃송이가
방긋방긋 웃으며
향기를 살며시
선사합니다.

Fragrance of White Rose

The white roses in garden
Are so beautiful
That the wind comes
And the sun visits

The white rose
Meets them with smile
Treats them
With fragrance.

맛있는 청포도

동글동글 연두알
알알이 맺어
주저리주저리
넓은 잎 달고
익어가는 초록알

송알송알 주저리
탱글탱글 터질 듯
맵시와 향기로
나를 꾀는 청포도
정말 맛있겠다.

Delicious Green Grapes

Tiny round light green balls
in clusters
Hanging on the vines
With broad leaves
Are ripening as green marbles.

In drops and drops,
Clusters and clusters,
Firm and bouncy,
Green grapes tempting me
Look delicious.

여행하는 철새

살기 좋은 곳 찾아
수천 리 멀다 않고
날아오는 철새들

계절 따라
찾아오는 길
잊어버리지 않네

지도도 보지 않고
그 먼 길 찾아오는
철새들은
기억력이 천재야!

Travelling Migratory Birds

For a better environment
Disregarding thousands of miles
The migratory birds fly back.

When it is the season
They come
Without fail.

Without a world map
They come that far.
The migration birds
Are all genius.

함박눈 내린 날

함박눈 내린 날
하얀 눈세상 되었다
달리던 자동차들
엉금엉금 조심조심

우리 가족 오빠 언니
눈 온 세상에서
살 수 없을까
조심조심하면서
서로 도와주니까.

Snowy Day

On a snowy day
Whole world became white.
The cars
They used to run so fast
Move slowly and slowly to be careful.

Can't my family,
My brother and sister,
Live in a snow world?
Then we will live
Using caution to be safe.

코스모스는

은빛 억새가
손짓하면
서산에 노을이
수줍은 양 얼굴 붉히고

코스모스는 가을이 좋아
하하하 호호호
그 고운 입을
다물지 못하고

산자락은
크레파스 칠한
그림 한 폭 주네.

Cosmos

When silver grass
Waves their hands
The twilight over the west mountain
Is shy and blushed its face.

Happy cosmos with autumn
Laugh, Ha, ha, ha ho, ho, ho.
They can't close
Their beautiful mouths.

Hills
Give me a piece of picture
Colored with crayons.

2부

빗방울은 예술

Part 2

Raindrop is Art

청개구리

귀여운 청개구리
꽥 꽥 꽥 울면
촉촉하게 보슬보슬
비가 내린다

조그만 청개구리
졸졸졸 맑은 물
흐르는 곳에
엄마 개구리 찾는가?

꽥 꽥 꽥
어린 청개구리
등이 차가운지
나뭇잎 밑에 숨네.

Green Frog

Ribbit, ribbit, ribbit,
When a tiny green frog
Croaks
The rain falls.

The green frog
Looks for mom
In where
Babbling clear water flows.

Ribbit, ribbit, ribbit,
The pretty green frog
Hides under a tree leaf.
His back may be cold.

아기 웃음은 행복

아가야 방실방실
꽃송이 우리 아가야

날마다 방실방실
우리 가족 행복이죠

응애응애 울어도
귀여워서 하하하

우리 가족 웃음 주고
행복 주는 아가야

Baby's Laughter is Happiness

Smile, our baby.
You are a flower bud.

Smile everyday.
You make my family happy

"Waa, waa" even though you cries
"Ha, ha, ha" what a cute baby.

You are a laughter storage
Giving my family happiness.

꽃잎들 여행

예쁜 꽃송이 송이는
나풀나풀 춤추며
바람 따라 향기는
날아 날아 날아서

벌 친구 나비 친구
윙윙윙 인사하며
달콤한 꿀 따고
꽃편지 읽고

씨앗들에게 안녕
인사하고
꽃잎들은 나풀나풀
여행 떠나지요.

Trip of Flower Petals

When beautiful flowers
Dance joyfully
The fragrance flies, flies
By the wing of wind.

Friendly bees and butterflies
Greet one anther, buzz, buzz, buzz
They collect sweet honey
And read the flower letters.

Saying goodbye to the seeds
The petals
Takc a trip.

자연이 주는 선물

자연은
사계절
우리에게
주는 선물이 있다

아름다운 꽃과
푸른 초원
맑은 물과 공기
지저귀는 새소리

풍성한 곡식과
맛있는 과일 열매 채소
자연이 주는
고마운 선물!

A Gift from Nature

Nature
Gives us
Gifts
Every season.

The beautiful flowers,
The green field,
The clear water and clean air
And chirping of birds.

Abundant grains,
Delicious fruits and vegetables
Thc grateful gifts
From nature

백목련 활짝 웃고

삼월 바람은
해님과 같이
눈 덮인 얼음산 녹이고

벌써 매화 향기에
산수유 진달래
노란 개나리
할미꽃 민들레 배시시 눈을 뜨고

백목련 활짝 웃고
수선화 수줍게 고개 숙여
인사하네, 고맙다고…….

White Magnolia Smiles

Wind of March
With Sun
Melts snow covered icy mountains.

Early fragrance of plum makes
Corni, azalea
And yellow forsythia smile,
Granny flower and dandelion opening up eyes slowly

White magnolia smiles broadly,
Daffodil bends head and says
Thank you …….

빗방울은 예술

꽃잎에 내려앉은
빗방울은 예술이야
나뭇잎에 빗방울은
한 폭의 그림

흙 위에 빗방울
목욕물 되어
미세먼지 씻어주니
상쾌한 공기가 되네.

깨끗한 환경 만들고
목마른 풀과 나무
수많은 생명의
젖줄이 되고…….

Raindrop is Art

Raindrops on flower petals
Are the teardrops of flowers.
They draw pictures
On tree leaves.

Raindrops on dirt
Become the bath water
To wash away fine dust
And to keep fresh air.

You make environment cozily
And mom's milk
To thirsty trees, grass
And countless lives.

집 업고 다니는 달팽이

달팽이야 달팽이야
그 집 어디서 지었니?
참 잘 지었다

달팽이가 집 속에
쏙 들어가면
딱 맞춤집

달팽이야 달팽이야
왜 집을
짊어지고 다니니?

참으로 힘이 세구나
부드러운 몸을
보호하기 위해서라고?

House Carrying Snail

Snail, snail
Where did you get that house?
It's nice.

The snail
Crawls back into the house.
It is just fit to him.

Snail, snail
Why are you
Carrying your house on the back?

Strong you are.
Is it to protect
Your soft body?

향기로운 마음

친구 위해 돕는 일
고마운 마음
연꽃같이 향기롭고
아름다운 마음

선생님 칭찬 말씀에
싱글벙글 웃음이 가득
서로서로 돕는 마음
향기로운 마음.

Fragrant Mind

The mind of helping friends
Is the brightly shinning mind.
It's fragrant and beautiful
Like a lotus flower.

By winning teacher's praise
We wear broad smiles on faces.
Helping one another
The fragrant mind.

꿈을 꾸는 꽃씨

꽃씨는
꿈속에서
벌 나비와 함께 노는
꿈을 꾸어요

작은 꽃씨는
향기를 만들고
방긋방긋 웃는
꿈을 꾸어요

A Dreaming Flower Seed

A flower seed
Dreams of a dream,
Playing with bees
And butterflies

A small flower seed
Dreams of a dream
Of making fragrance
And cracking smiles.

다정한 친구

내가 먼저 인사하는
밝고 맑은 마음
좋은 친구가 되고 싶다

따뜻하고 정답게
배려하고 양보하면
다정한 친구 되지.

Close Friend

I want to be a good friend to you
By having bright crystal mind
And saying hi first

Lets be close friends
By having warm hearts
And caring each other.

바람은 택배 아저씨

금물결 은물결 파도 타고
바람이 넘실넘실
육지로 놀러오면

꽃바람 되어 들과 산에
나풀나풀 놀다가
어린 새싹 잠 깨우고

논밭으로 계곡으로
지친 듯 살랑살랑
나뭇잎에 앉아 그네도 타고

흙 냄새 땀 냄새도
어디로 싣고 가는지
바람은 택배 아저씨!

Wind is a Delivery Man

In a sea when the wind surfs
The gold waves and silver waves
Visit to the land.

In fields and mountains
The flowery wind runs around
To awake sleeping new spouts.

In the rice paddies and valleys
The tired wind
Sits on a leaf to swing.

Where do you carry
The dirt smell and sweat smell
Mr. Wind, the deliver-man!

바다의 날, 5월 31일

끝없이 넓은 푸른 바다
아름다운 생명의 시가 있고
아낌없이 다 주는 깊고 넓은
풍요로운 어머니 같은 바다

풍족하고 넉넉한 바다
5월 31일은 바다의 날
지구를 안고 세계문화를
교류하는 아버지 같은 바다

May 31st, The Day of Sea

The broad and wide blue sea
Serves us with beautiful vital poems.
A generous mother-like
Deep and wide sea gives away everything.

Rich and abundant sea.
May 31st is Marine Day.
A father-like sea
Hugs Earth and helps cultural exchange in the world.

3부

5월의 초록빛

Part 3

Green in May

자연이 주는 사랑

자연환경이
우리에게 사랑을 주네
시원한 바람과 물
밝고 따뜻한 빛
숨 쉴 수 있는 맑은 공기
편안히 살 수 있는 땅

자연환경이
우리에게 사랑을 주네
깨끗이 사용하여
우리가 머문 자리 살펴보고
다음 사람이 기뻐하도록
잘 넘겨줘야지.

Love from the Nature

Earth environment
Gives us love.
Cool wind and water,
Bright and warm light,
Clean air breathing,
And land we can live in peace

Earth environment
Gives us love.
Let's use it carefully.
Let's look back the place we've stayed.
To make next generation happy
We should hand it over in good condition.

가을이 오는 소리

고요한 밤
내 책상에서 들리는
귀뚜라미 연주

왜적을 물리친
이순신 장군 위인전
책장을 넘긴다

바람이 시원하다
가을이 오는 소리!

Stepping Sound of Autumn

In a silent night
Cricket music
Reached my desk.

I turned the pages.
Of book of Admiral Yi Sunsin
Who defeated the invaded Japanese

Wind is cool
The sound of coming autumn!

춤추는 알밤

귀뚜라미 연주 소리에
가을바람이
가시밤송이와 춤을 추네

발그레한 예쁜 알밤
툭툭툭 여기 저기
풀 속으로 뛰어내리네

나 여기 있지
알밤이 숨바꼭질하자네.

Dancing Chestnuts

In the rhythm of cricket's play
Autumn wind
Dances with a thorny chestnut bur.

Tap, tap, tap,
Ruddy and pretty chestnuts
Jump down into grass.

I am here.
Chestnuts want the hide and seek game.

가을 댓잎들 이야기

댓잎들이 깔깔깔
바람과 춤추며
사각사각 소란스럽다

산에는 붉은 단풍
들판에는 황금색
오곡백과 풍성한데

곧
찬 서리에 국화 향기 그윽하면
창공에 기러기 철새들
줄지어 날아가겠지.

Autumn Bamboo Leaves Talk

The bamboo leaves
Dance with wind
Rustle! rustle!

In the mountains red colored leaves,
In the field gold colors,
Abundant grains and fruits.

Soon
By cold frost the mum flowers emit fragrance,
The wild gees and other migration birds in blue sky
Will fly in formations.

의좋은 사형제

해는 어둠을 밝혀
따뜻함을 주고

흙은 모든 생명의
보금자리 되고

물은 낮은 곳으로
흘러흘러
바다가 되고

바람은 넉넉한 마음
계절마다 소식과 지혜 주는

해
흙
바다
바람
의좋은 사형제!

Four Good Brothers

Sun light up in darkness
And gives us warmth.

Dirt becomes
Nests to all lives.

Water toward lower ground
Flow, flow
To become the sea

Wind with its generous mind
Gives good news and wisdom every season.

Sun
Dirt
Sea
Wind
The four good brothers!

눈 오는 날

하늘에서 하얀 눈이
펄펄 내리고
땅에는 소복소복
눈이 쌓이고
어느새 온 세상이
눈나라 만들었네

아버지는 눈길을 만들고
오빠와 동생은
눈사람 만들고
바둑이는 꼬리 치며
뛰뛰기 하네

눈 오는 날은
온 세상이
축복이라네.

Snowing Day

Lovely snow
Fly down from the sky.
Snow pile is growing
On the ground.
White snow flakes
Build a snow kingdom.

Dad makes a road on the snow.
Brother and sister together
Make a snowman.
Our excited puppy
Jumps around here and there.

Snowing day
The day
Whole world is blessed.

계절은 친구다

한겨울 바람이
쌩쌩쌩 불어올 때
추위가
친구 되었네

3월이 오면
추위는 가고
따스한 봄볕
가만히 속삭이네.

Seasons are my Friends

When cold winter wind
Blows whoosh, whoosh, whoosh
The cold
Becomes my friend

When March comes
Cold is gone,
Warm spring sunlight
Whispers to me.

자연이 먼저 알아요

쓰레기 되기 전 모습은
모두가 소중한 자원

내 모습 소중하듯
아껴 쓰고 귀히 여기며

쓰레기 줄이는
아름다운 생활

그 마음 그 모습 그 사랑은
자연이 먼저 알아요.

Nature Knows Already

Before being a trash
Everything is an important resource.

As much as you love yourself
Love other things too.

Life of less trash
Will get applause from whole world.

That mind, that attitudes and that love
The Nature knows already.

동대구역 겨울 비둘기

구구구 구구구
포르르 날아날아 내린다
동대구역 플랫폼
선로 위를 작은 두 발로
아장아장 걸어걸어
먹이 찾아다니는 비둘기 한 쌍!

고개 돌려 무서움도 잊은 채
부지런히 주워 먹는
먹이 부스러기들
회색빛 바닥에
발이 시려 한쪽 발
가슴에 올려다 내린다
동대구역 겨울 비둘기 한 쌍!

Winer Dove at Dongdaegu Station

Coo, coo, coo, coo, coo, coo,
A dove fly down gently
At Dongdaegu Station platform.
With frozen bare feet.
It toddles on the rail
To look for feed.

Ignoring fear by facing away
It is busy with picking up feed
The crumbs of life.
On grey concrete floor
It lifts up its frozen feet
To chest and down
A couple of doves!

초록빛 오월은

산과 들은
푸른 초원
새들이 노래하고

나뭇잎들은
해님과 소곤소곤

풀잎은
야들야들 보들보들
벌레들의 집이 되네.

초록빛
오월은.

Green in May

In hills and fields
Green grass
And birds sing

Tree leaves
Whisper with sun

Grasses,
Tender and soft,
Good for insects' nests.

Green
May.

꽃처럼 고운 마음

이른 아침 학교 울타리에
노란 개나리꽃 방글방글
참새들 폴폴폴 날아와
예쁜 꽃가지에 앉았네

봄소식을 알리느라
짹짹짹 지저귀는 새소리
나도 으음음 저절로 콧노래
꽃처럼 고운 마음 활짝…….

Flowery Mind

In early morning the golden bell flowers
Of school fence are smiling.
The sparrows fly in
To sit on the beautiful flower branches.

To announce the spring news
Chirp, chirp, chirp, the birds talk.
Hum, hum, I hum without I knowing it,
Flowery mind is opened widely….

4부

청개구리
구슬 세는 날

Part 4

The Day the Green Frog Counts the Marbles

춤추는 바다

끝없이 펼쳐진
푸른 비단 바다
해님 달님 빛바늘로
금물결 은물결
수를 놓으며
갈매기처럼 춤추고

고기잡이배들은
길고 긴 비단 한 필
풀어놓은
바닷길 위로
넘실넘실 넘실넘실
만선의 춤을 춰요.

Dancing Sea

In endlessly spreaded
Blue silk sea
Sun and Moon embroider
Gold waves and silver waves
With light needles.
They dance joyfully
Like sea gulls.

Fishing boats
On the long and long
Silk strip
Of sea road
Dance joyfully
For the full loads of fish.

아름다운 미소

잔디의 미소는
연초록 마음

꽃들의 미소는
그윽한 향기

바람의 미소는
춤추는 잎새들

아이들의 미소는
밝은 얼굴이지요.

Beautiful Smile

The smile of wind
The green spirit.

The smile of flowers
The sweet fragrance.

The smile of wind
The dancing grass.

The smile of children
The happy faces.

아기 눈엔

모든 것
다 볼 수 있대요
엄마 아빠가
아기 눈에 있대요

알아보고
방긋방긋
꽃송이 아기 눈에
모두가 있어요.

Baby's Eyes

Everything
Is in baby's eyes.
Mommy and Daddy
Are in his eyes.

Smile
At familiar faces.
Everybody is
In flowery baby's eyes.

구름 운동회

파란 하늘 운동장에
흰 유니폼 구름선수들
응원전은 번쩍번쩍
양떼들이 방실방실
운동회가 시작되었다

양떼구름은 동쪽에서
뭉게구름 서쪽에서
번개신호가 번쩍
호루라기 천둥이
우르르르 쾅쾅쾅
신나게 달리는 구름들

양떼구름이 앞장서서
웃통 벗어 던지며
뭉게구름을 제치고
일등으로 달린다
햇빛 만국기에
바람도 너울너울 춤추네.

Sports Day of Clouds

In blue sky school ground
Cloud players in white uniforms,
Flashing lights of cheering,
Smiling flock of sheep,
The sports day opened

A proud black clouds,
A hopping fleecy cloud
And the smiling lambs
Begin the sports day
In loud cheers.

The sheep clouds in the east,
The fleecy cloud in the west,
Flashing light of start signal,
The whistle thunder roars
"Krrr... Blam! blam! blam!"
The clouds run fast.

A sheep cloud ahead
Takes off his top and throw away,
Passes fleecy cloud
And Runs first place.
Sunshine national flags are flagging.
Wind is joyfully dancing.

선물 주는 가을

가을이 주는 선물은
들녘에 황금물결
벼 이삭이 고개 숙이며
땀 흘린 겸손함
찬 서리에 울긋불긋
빨간 단풍 노란 단풍
맛있는 과일과 열매들
참 고마운 자연의 은혜로움

Gift from Autumn

Gift from autumn is
Golden wave in the field.
Rice ears head down politely
After sweating hard.
Cold frost paints
Red maples and yellow maples,
Delicious fruits and berries
How grateful the nature is.

옥상에 자란 개망초

바람에 날아온 풀씨가
메마른 옥상에서
뿌리 내리고 자랐네

먼지를 친구하여
빗물 흐르는 곳에
뿌리를 뻗었네

별들이 반짝반짝
밤이슬 내려주는
사랑받아 꽃을 피웠네

개망초 너는 스스로
살아가는 힘
보여주어 고맙다, 사랑해!

Daisy Fleabane on Rooftop

A daisy fleabane seed blown down by wind,
Rooted and grew up
On the barren rooftop.

Keeping friendship with dust
It stretched roots
To the place where rainwater flows.

With love of shining stars
The night dew
Bloomed flowers

Daisy fleabane,
You show us how to survive by oneself.
Thank you and love you.

솔방울이 웃는 날

솔방울 방울들이
향긋한 씨앗을 품고
사계절을 하루같이
큰 꿈을 키워요.

맑은 가을바람이
파란 바늘잎 쓰다듬으면
솔방울이 좋아서
꿈을 안고 날아내려요.

The Day The Pine Corns Laugh

Pine corns have blue dreams
Of living four seasons in green.
They dream of big dreams
Everyday in four seasons

When fresh autumn wind
Pets the green needles
The pine seeds jump out of corns
To the ground
With dreams of being the big pine trees.

행복 주는 아기 동생

학교 갔다 오면
날마다 방실방실
웃음 주는 재롱둥이

내 아기 동생은
잠을 잘 때도
방긋방긋 웃고

아침해 뜨면
해처럼 웃으며
행복 주는 아기 동생

My Baby Brother Gives us Happiness

When I come home after school
My cute baby brother
Smiles at me brightly.

My little brother
Smiles
Even while he is sleeping.

When sun rises
He smiles like the sun.
My baby brother is a happiness giver.

할아버지 고향

조용한 시골마을
양지바른 남향집이
할아버지 고향 할아버지 집
앞산엔 고운 진달래
산새들의 정다운 노래 들으며
보리밭 이랑이 춤추는 곳

하늘에 뭉게구름 피어오르면
일기예보 맞추는 할아버지
옆집 순복이엄마 효부상 받고
앞집 손자 동동이 판사 되어
온 동네 축하잔치로 행복한 날
전설이 숨 쉬는 할아버지 고향

Grandpa's Home

In a quiet country
A Warm house facing south
My grandpa's home.
Where beautiful azaleas are in front hill,
Mountain birds sing merrily
And barley in the field dance.

If fleecy clouds rise in the sky
My grandma foretells rain.
Sunbok's mom of next door won the prize of Good Daughter-in-Law.
Grandson of front house became a judge.
What the happy days for the village folks.
Legend is alive here.

자연의 힘

자연은 우리에게
사랑의 균형을 만들어
환경을 아름답게 하고
계절은 즐거움을 준다

지구촌에 힘이 되어
평화롭고 행복하게
빛과 바람 물 공기
다 주는 자연의 힘.

Power of Nature

Nature keeps balance
Among loves
To keep environment beautiful,
To keep joyful seasons.

To encourages global village,
To be peaceful and happy,
The power of nature
Gives us light, wind, water and air.

청개구리 구슬 세는 날

넓은 연잎 위에 앉아서
파란 청개구리 꿱꿱꿱
빗방울 구슬 세고 있네

둥근 눈망울 굴리면서
톡톡 또르르 또르르르
청개구리 은구슬 치는 날

참 재미있겠다.

The Day the Green Frog Counts the Marbles

Ribbet, ribbet, ribbet.
Sitting on a broad lotus leaf
The green frog counts the marbles.

Rolling its big and round eyes
For the green frog
It's the day of playing marbles.

Oh, what a fun.

5부

가을이 주는 선물

Part 5

Present from Autumn

우리 집 가족 사랑

할아버지 할머니는
아빠의 아버지 어머니
고모 삼촌은 아빠의
여동생 남동생

엄마의 큰딸은 나의 언니
아들은 나의 오빠
나는 막내딸
우리 가족은 아홉 사람

서로서로 도우며
웃음으로 살아요
고모 시집가고
삼촌 장가가면
가족 사랑
내가 제일 많이 받을거야.

Family Love of our Home

Grandpa's grandma is
My father's father's mother.
Aunt and uncle are
My father's sister and brother.

Mother's daughter is my sister,
Her son is my brother
And I am the youngest daughter.
My family member is nine

We live with smiles
While helping one another.
If my aunt marry off
And if my uncle makes his own home
I will be in the center
Of my family love.

귀여운 아가는

응애 응애 응애
귀여운 아가는
엄마 부르고

응애 응애 응애
예쁜 아가는
엄마 젖 빨고

응애 응애 응애
기저귀 바꿔주는
엄마 보며

방긋방긋 생글생글
나도 저렇게
자랐을 거야.

Cute Baby

Waa, waa, waa.
Cute baby
Calls mom.

Waa, waa, waa.
Pretty baby
Wants mom's milk.

Waa, waa, waa.
At mom
For changing his diaper.

Sweet and broad smiles.
Wonder if I grew
That way too.

단짝

햇볕처럼 따스하고
눈으로도 말하는
맑은 공기 같은 친구

잘못하면 꾸짖어 주고
힘들어할 때 도와주며
비 오는 날 우산 같은 친구

도시락 나눠먹으며
바늘에 실 같은
하늘에 달 같은 친구

My Close Friend

My close friend is warm like the sun,
He talks with his eyes.
He is as clean as air.

He advises me for my wrong doings,
Offers helping hand for my troubles
He is like an umbrella on rainy days.

He and I share the same lunch box,
We are a needle and thread.
He is like a moon in the sky.

93회 전국체육대회

맘이 설레요
몸을 앞뒤 좌우로 움직여요
뜻한 바대로 이루어지길 바라요

달콤한 열매보다 쓴 인내로
구차한 변명보다 확실한 결과로
벌써 대구에는
에너지로 넘쳐나요
서로서로 기쁨과 고통을 나눠요

하나가 되어가는 93회 전국체육대회
나로 태어나 우리가 되어가는 이 시간
노력의 결과는 빛이 될 거예요.

The 93rd National Sports Festival

We are excited.
Move your body forward, backward, to left, to right.
Hope you achieve as you expected.

A bitter patient than a sweet fruit.
An honest result than a poor excuse.
Daegu is already
Overwhelming with energy.
Let's share all joys and pains.

We are one in the 93rd National Sports Festival.
'I' becomes 'we' during this time.
Our efforts will be resulted as a bright light.

가을 낙동강

반짝반짝 은비늘 금비늘
물너울 잉어 떼를
거슬러 올라가
노을빛 담고 흐르는
가을 낙동강

곱게 차려입은 단풍산 담아
굽이굽이 돌아서
갈대들의 박수 받으며
바다로 여행하는
가을 낙동강

Nakdong River in Autumn

Glistening their silver and gold scales
A school of catfishes
Swim upstream.
Autumn Nakdong River
Flows with autumn scenery.

Carrying colorfully dressed up autumn hills,
Flowing along every bends
And getting big hand from weeds
The autumn Nakdong River
Travels to sea.

깊어가는 가을

이산 저산 빨간 단풍
고운 감나무잎
들에도 황금물결
축제가 열렸다

귀뚜라미 연주에
깊어가는 가을
어머니 고운 스카프
사드리고 싶다.

Late Autumn

Red autumn leaves in this and that hills,
Beautiful persimmon tree leaves,
Golden waves in the field,
A festival is held.

With concert of crickets
Autumn is deepened.
I want to buy a beautiful scarf
For my mother.

결실의 계절

동글동글 까만 씨앗
사랑스런 곡식 열매
조롱조롱 탐스런 과일
시원한 바람에
춤추는 황금물결

가을은 아쉬움 주는 계절
마법의 요술쟁이
아름다운 가을
독서하기 좋은 계절
결실의 계절

Fruiting Season

Round and shining seeds,
Lovely grains,
Cute and beautiful fruits
With cool wind
Golden waves dance.

Autumn gives sorrow
While it is a magician.
A beautiful season,
Good for book reading
And a fruiting season.

참새 쫓는 허수아비

가을 들녘
너울대는 황금물결
참새 떼 쫓는
허수아비 두 팔
더덩실 덩실
바람에 어깨춤 추네
밀짚모자에
까매진 얼굴
허이 허어이
참새 떼 날아가네.

Scarecrow for Sparrows

In autumn field
Of dancing golden waves,
A scarecrow for sparrows
Extending its arms
Dances a shoulder dance joyfully
To the rhythm of wind.
Under the straw hat
The sunburned face
Whoopee...!
The sparrows fly away.

우산 쓴 코스모스

길가에 코스모스
바람에 살랑살랑
실같이 가느다란
잎줄기에 간들간들

빨간 하얀 분홍 우산 쓰고
쓰러질 듯 쓰러질 듯
비바람에 무용하는
예쁜 코스모스.

Cosmos Under Umbrellas

Cosmos beside a road
Dance in wind.
Thread like thin bodies
Sway on and on.

Holding red white pink umbrellas
And swaying almost to the ground
To the rhythm of rainstorm
The cosmos dance.

책의 힘

책 속에는
훌륭한 사람이 가득
열심히 노력하여
본받고 싶다

사람의 향기 가득한
책의 힘

그래서 누군가
이런 말을 했지

"총을 이기는 건 펜이다."

Power of Book

In the books
There are many great people.
I will be like them
With great efforts.

Power of books
Full of men's fragrance

So someone
Once said

"A pen wins a gun"

눈꽃

하늘에서 하얀 눈이
폴폴폴 날아날아
내리는 꽃잎처럼
아름답게 피어나네

푸른 동백나무에도
조롱조롱 열매처럼
산과 들 집에도
송이송이 달렸네.

Snow Flakes

From the sky
White snow flakes
Fall and fall
To bloom beautiful flowers.

Green camellia
Got ice berries.
Hills, fields and houses
Got ice berries.

자연 속에 살면서 환경을 생각하게 합니다

1. 권대자 시인에 대하여

아동문학가 · 시인 권대자 선생님은 2014년 4월에 다섯 번째 동시집 『자연이 주는 이야기』를 내셨습니다. 그러니 이번에 출간한 이 동시집은 여섯 번째로 내는 책입니다.

『청개구리 구슬 세는 날』 참 재미있지요?

선생님은 대구시 동구의 한 산자락에 '도동시비공원'을 마련하고 많은 시인과 동시인들의 시비(문학비)를 건립하면서 자연과 환경 운동에 앞장서 일하고 계시는 분입니다.

남들은 땅이 있으면 공장이나 아파트 같은 큰 건물을 짓는다고 야단인데, 권대자 시인은 아름다운 자연을 그대로 보전하면서 맑고 깨끗한 환경을 가꾸는 일과, 그런 것을 소재로 시와 동시를 쓰는 분이십니다.

요즘 우리나라는 생각지도 않은 '미세먼지' 때문에 숨 쉬는 일마저 어려워지고 있잖아요. 옛날에는 생각지도 못했던 일입니다.

권대자 선생님은 우리가 살아가면서 자연 훼손 때문에 고통받는 일에 대하여 몹시 안타까워하시고 자연과 환경보호운동에 힘을 기울이고 계시는 고마운 분입니다.

2. '청개구리 구슬 세는 날'은 어떤 동시일까요?

책 이름으로 붙여진 이 동시부터 살펴보겠습니다.

> 넓은 연잎 위에 앉아서
> 파란 청개구리 퀙퀙퀙
> 빗방울 구슬 세고 있네
>
> 둥근 눈망울 굴리면서
> 톡톡 또르르 또르르르
> 청개구리 은구슬 치는 날
>
> 참 재미있겠다.
>
> —「청개구리 구슬 세는 날」 전문

이 동시는 3연 7행으로 비교적 짧은 시입니다.

첫 연에서 '넓은 연잎 위에 앉아서/파란 청개구리 퀙퀙퀙/빗방울 구슬 세고 있네' 하고 지은이가 연잎 위에 동그마니 앉아 있는 청개구리를 어떤 모습으로 보고 있나요? 빗방울이 한 방울 떨어질 때마다 그것을 구슬로 보고 있다는 사실입니다. 그런데 무엇보다 빗방울이 방울져 떨어질 때 청개구리는 가만히 있지 않고 무슨 소리를 내는 겁니다. '퀙!' 하는 소리지요.

이것을 권대자 시인은 청개구리와 교감하면서 '퀙'은 청개구리의 구슬 세는 소리로 느끼고 있습니다. 얼마나 재미있는 상상입니까?

둘째 연은 더욱 재미있는 상상이지요. 청개구리는 큰 눈망울을 굴리면서 '톡톡 또르르 또르르르' 물방울인 은구슬을 마치 어린들이 땅에서 구슬치기하듯 은구슬 친다는 생각을 펴고 있지요.

그러니 이 짧은 한 편의 동시 속에 얼마나 많은 동심의 이야기 세계가 펼쳐지고 있는지 짐작이 갈 것입니다.

마지막 셋째 연은 딱 한 줄 '참 재미있겠다.'란 시인의 생각 한마디로 마무리되었습니다.

여기서 한 가지 덧붙이고 싶은 말은 「청개구리 구슬 세는 날」 같은 시는 동심을 지니고 있는 어린이들이나, 동심을 바탕으로 글을 쓰고 있는 아동문학가만이 쓸 수 있다고 하겠습니다.

3. 이 책의 많은 동시들은…

동시집의 차례에서 살펴보면 동시의 제목들이 크게 3가지로 구분되고 있습니다.

첫째는 아름다운 자연의 모습입니다.

「물소리와 꽃향기」「풀밭의 속삭임」「함박눈 내린 날」「빗방울은 예술」「자연이 주는 선물」 등 많은 동시가 그것입니다.

둘째는 사랑과 우정입니다. 사랑은 매우 광범위합니다. 자연의 사랑도 있고 사람이나 동식물의 사랑도 있습니다.

「학교 친구 내 짝꿍」「우리 집 가족 사랑」「여행하는 철새」「의좋은 사형제」「아기 웃음은 행복」「우산 쓴 코스모스」「동대구역 겨울 비둘기」 등 수없이 많습니다.

셋째는 생활의 즐거움을 꼽을 수 있습니다.

「독서는 즐거워」「눈 오는 날」「행복 주는 아기 동생」「할아버지 고향」「93회 전국체육대회」「단짝」「아기 눈엔」 등 많은 동시에서 삶의 보람과 즐거움을 느낄 수 있습니다.

이제 동시 세 편만 살펴보겠습니다.

산골은 깊어서
계곡물이 졸졸졸
얼음 속에서 흘러도
그 편안한 소리는
자연의 자장가

팔공산 봉우리에
흰 눈이 녹지 않아도
노란 산수유꽃
매화꽃 향기는
자연의 숨결

—「물소리와 꽃향기」 전문

첫째 연은 산골에서 흐르는 물소리를 대자연의 자장가로 비유했습니다. 그리고 둘째 연에서는 산속에 피고 있는 매화꽃, 산수유꽃 향기를 자연의 숨결로 비유하면서, 물소리와 꽃향기를 자연의 조화로움(아름다움)을 재미있게 노래하고 있답

니다.

다음은 '사랑과 우정'을 담고 있는 동시입니다.

길가에 코스모스
바람에 살랑살랑
실같이 가느다란
잎줄기에 간들간들

빨간 하얀 분홍 우산 쓰고
쓰러질 듯 쓰러질 듯
비바람에 무용하는
예쁜 코스모스.

—「우산 쓴 모스모스」 전문

길가에 늘어선 코스모스가 바람에 살랑대는 모습만 보아도 사랑스럽고 정겨움을 느낄 수 있지요.

빨간색, 분홍색, 하얀색의 꽃잎들이 마치 양산이나 우산을 쓴 것처럼 정겨움을 느낄 수 있는데 약간의 비바람에 마치 군무를 연상케하는 코스모스 예쁜 꽃들의 멋진 춤은 더욱 사랑스럽고 정겨운 우정을 짐작할 수 있답니다.

마지막 동시 한 편을 감상하겠습니다.

이 시는 생활(삶) 속의 즐거움을 연상하게 합니다.

하늘에서 하얀 눈이
펄펄 내리고
땅에는 소복소복
눈이 쌓이고

어느새 온 세상이
눈나라 만들었네

아버지는 눈길을 만들고
오빠와 동생은
눈사람 만들고
바둑이는 꼬리 치며
뛰뛰기 하네

눈 오는 날은
온 세상이
축복이라네.

—「눈 오는 날」 전문

눈이 내리면 어린들이 가장 좋아합니다. 같이 따라다니는 바둑이도 좋아 어쩔 줄 모릅니다. 아빠는 눈 가래로 눈길을 치면서도 아이들과 함께 좋아합니다.

이 광경이 삶 속의 즐거움입니다.

권대자 시인이 쓴 이 동시집은 모든 동시가 자연 사랑과 우리가 살아가는 환경보호와 그리고 우리 모두의 삶에 대한 즐거움, 보람을 노래하고 있음을 깊이 느끼게 됩니다.

좋은 동시집 탄생을 진심으로 축하합니다.

엄 기 원
(한국문인협회 고문 · 아동문학가)

It let us Think of Environment while Living in Nature

1. About Kwon Daeja

Kwon Daeja, a children poem writer and poetry, wrote The Stories from Nature, the fifth children poem book in April 2014. So, this children poem book is the sixth one.

Isn't interesting this book, *The day the Green Frog Counts the Marbles*?

Kwon Daeja is leading nature and environment protection movement. She constructed 'Dodong Poem Monuments Park' below a mountain in Donggu Daegu in which inscribed many poetries and children's poems of many poets and other children's poem writers.

Many people, if they have lands, may be busy to build factories or apartments but Kwon Daeja is different. She likes to keep nature as it is by promoting better nature and at the same time writing poems and children's poems with those data.

These days we have trouble in breathing because of fine dust which we never expected before. Mrs. Kwon is very sorry for that trouble.

Which are caused by nature destructions, and tries her best effort to protect the nature and environment.

2. What is the children's poem, The Day the Green Frog Counts the Marbles, like? We will study this poem, the title of this book.

Ribbet, ribbet, ribbet.
Sitting on a broad lotus leaf
The green frog counts the marbles.

Rolling its big and round eyes
For the green frog
It's the day of playing marbles.

Oh, what a fun.

<The Day the Green Frog Counts the Marbles>

It is a short children's poem with 3 verses and 7 lines.

In the first verse, 'Sitting on a broad lotus leaf, the green frog counts the marbles.' What does it look like to the writer the scene of

the frog sitting on a lotus leaf? She sees the rain drops as marbles. The frog does not just look at them in silence. It makes sound, ribbet! The poet hears the frog's sound, ribbet, as the frog is counting marbles. How amazing imagination!

The second verse is more amazing. The frog's big rolling eyeballs reminds the poet the children playing marbles.

By this way, she stored a lot of stories of children's innocent mind in this short poem.

Last verse, 'what a fun,' is short but well described the poet's condensed thought.

In addition, I can say that the idea, 'The day the Green Frog Counts the Marbles' can only be produced from children or children's poem writers.

3. Many children's poems in this book……

The titles of her childrens poems in the content can be classified into three.

First, the features of beautiful nature.

'The Flowing Water Sound and the Flower Fragrance', 'Whispering from the Grass Field', 'Snowy Day', 'Raindrop is Art' and 'A Gift from Nature'.

Second, Love and friendship.

There are many kinds of love, such as love of nature, and love of people and animals. As friendship, there are 'My School Seating

Mate', 'Family Love of our Home', 'Travelling Migratory Birds' and 'Four Good Brothers', 'Baby's Laughter is Happiness', 'Cosmos Under Umbrellas' and 'Winter Dove at Dongdaegu Station' and some others.

Third, happy life.

'Book Reading is Fun', 'Snowy Day', 'My Baby Brother Gives us Happiness', 'Grandpa's Home', 'The 93rd National Sports Festival', 'My close Friend', 'Baby's Eyes' and others. Those poems make us to feel the worth and pleasure of life.

Now we will see three more children's poems.

Trickling, trickling, trickling,
The sound of flowing water
Under ice in a brook
Is the sweet lullaby
Of the Mother of Nature.

Even though the head of Palgong Mountain
Is white with snow
The yellow corni flowers
And the fragrance of plum blossoms
Are the breath of nature.

<The Flowing Water Sound and the Flower Fragrance>

In the first verse, water flowing sound is metaphor of lullaby from the Mother Nature. In second verse, the fragrance of plum and corni.

Flowers are metaphor of the breath of Mother Nature. By describing so, the poet admires the harmony between water sound and flower fragrance in nature.

The second one is about love and friendship.

Cosmos beside a road
Dance in wind.
Thread like thin bodies
Sway on and on.

Holding red white pink umbrellas
And swaying almost to the ground
To the rhythm of rainstorm
The cosmos dance.

<Cosmos Under Umbrellas>

Everybody loves the shaking cosmos by wind beside roadsides. Red, ping and white flower petals look like beautiful parasols or umbrellas. Their shaking feature of cosmos by wind reminds us a group dance with friends or a strong friendship.

We will see one more poem for the last. This poem reminds us the pleasure in our lives.

Lovely snow
Fly down from the sky.
Snow pile is growing
On the ground.
White snow flakes

Build a snow kingdom.

Dad makes a road on the snow.
Brother and sister together
Make a snowman.
Our excited puppy
Jumps around here and there.

Snowing day
The day of
Whole world is blessed

<Snowing Day>

Children like snowing days the best. Puppies come along the children are excited. Fathers who make roads with snow spades are also joyful with children.

This is the scene of happiness in our lives.

The poet Kown Daeja reminds us, through her poems the love of Mother Nature, the importance of environment protection and the happiness of our lives.

I truly congratulate the birth of this wonderful children's poem collection.

EOM, Kiwon

(Advisor of Korea Writers Association and
Children's Poem Writer)

| 시인 | **권대자**

- 1942년 경북 안동 출생
- 대구문인협회 등단(2002년)
- 《문학예술》 신인문학상(동시 부분) 수상(2006년)
- 도동시비동산 건립(2007년)
- 영남아동문학상 수상(2009년)
- 대구예술상(문학 부문) 수상(2011년)
- 한국아동문학 창작상 수상(2014년)

- 도동시비동산 운영위원장
- 영남아동문학회 부회장
- 한국아동문학연구회 부회장
- 문학예술가협회 대구경북 이사
- PEN문학 회원
- 대구문인협회 전(前) 부회장
- 한국문인협회 회원 및 한국아동문학회 회원
- 한국동시문학회 회원
- 한국불교아동문학회 이사
- 반짇고리문학회 회장
- 대구여성문학회 회원

□ 작품집
- 환경동시집 『세상은 자연』 출간(2002년)
- 환경동시집 『풀꽃사랑』 출간(2004년)
- 동시집 『구슬빗방울』 출간(2007년)
- 동시집 『손뼉 치는 바다』 출간(2009년)
- 동시집 『자연이 주는 이야기』 출간(2014년)
- 동시집 『청개구리 구슬 세는 날』 출간(2019년)

□ 주소 : (41029) 대구광역시 동구 팔공로33길 6(불로동)
□ 연락처 : 010-6567-3363
□ E-mal : kbk3030@naver.com

| Poet | KWON, Daeja

- Born in Andong in 1942
- Joined Daegu Literator Association in 2002
- New Literator Award (Children's Poem) of Literary Art in 2006
- Built Dodong Poem Monument in 2007
- Yeongnam Children Literature Award in 2009
- Daegu Art Award (Literature) in 2011
- Creative Writing Award of Korean Children Literature in 2014

- Manager of Dodong Poem Monument Hill
- Vice President of Yeongnam Children Literature Association
- Vice President of Korean Children Literature Research Association
- Director of Daegu Gyeongbuk Literary Art Association
- Member of PEN Literature
- Vice President (Former) of Daegu Literator Association
- Member of Korean Literator Association and Korean Children Literature Association
- Member of Korean Children Literature Association
- Director of Korean Buddhism Children Literature Association
- President of Banjitgori
- Member of Daegu Women Literator Association

□ Literary Work

- Environmental Children Poem 『World is Nature』 in 2002
- Environmental Children Poem 『Grass Flower Love』 in 2002
- Children Poem 『Marble Rain Drops』 in 2007
- Children Poem 『Clapping Sea』 in 2009
- Children Poem 『Stories from Nature』 in 2014
- Children Poem 『The Day the Green Frog Counts the Marbles』 in 2019

□ Address : 6, Palgong-ro 33-gil, Dong-gu, Daegu, Korea
□ Phone : 010-6567-3363
□ E-mail : kbk3030@naver.com

| 번역 | **진철보**(陳哲補)

- 계명대학교 교육대학원 영어교육과 졸업 (석사)
- 1974. 4~2007. 10. 대구미국인학교 교사(한국문화사/한국어)
- 1980. 3~1984. 2. 대구대학교경상대 관광학과 영어강사
- 1984. 4~1995. 6. 대구 LIKE/ECA/대덕문화원 수석영어강사
- 1992. 3~2005. 8. 대구 및 경북교원연수원 초청강사
- 2007. 9~2009. 3. 충북 영동군(부영/황간/구룡 초등학교) 영어센터장 영어교사 및 원어민 코디네이터
- 2009. 1~2010. 5. 잉글리쉬 무무 독해교재, iBT 영어독해교재 집필
- 2011. 4~현재 (대구)삼성이주공사 사무국장 국제행정영문전담

□ 저서

- 1989. 8. The Grateful Magpie(한국전래동화), 서울국제출판사
- 1994. 8. It's for You 1,2,3권(영어회화교재), Unibooks 출판사
- 1996. 10. Five Hint Quiz(영어 퀴즈), 아카데미 출판사
- 2003. 11. The Royal Inspector and the Masked Dance(독해교재) 튼튼영어사
- 2009. 1. 영어독해교재 (잉글리쉬 무무사) 40권 iBT 초급독해교재 6권

□ 주소 : 대구시 중구 명륜로 26길 53-2
□ 연락처 : 010-9050-2834

| Translator | JIN, Cheolbo

- 1974/4~2007/10 Korean Culture Teacher of Daegu American School
- 1980/3~1984/2 English Lecturer at Daegu University Tourism Dept.
- 1992/3~2005/8 English Lecturer at Daegu & Gyeongbuk Teachers Education Center
- 2009/1~2010/5 Reading Textbook Writer for English MuMu/iBT
- 2011/4~Present (Daegu) Samsung Emigration Office International Administration Dept.

□ Author of

- 1989/8 The Grateful Magpie (Korean Folk Tale) - Seoul International Printing Co.
- 1994/8 It's for You book 1,2,3 (English Conversation)-Unibooks
- 1996/10 Five Hint Quiz (English Quiz) - Academy Printing Co.
- 2003/11 The Royal Inspector & the Masked Dancer (Reading) TeunTeun English Co.
- 2009/1 Intensive English Reading books 40 volumes(English MuMu) and iBT Reading books 6 volumes

□ Address : 53-2, Myeongryun-ro 26-gil, Jung-gu, Daegu, Korea
□ Phone : 010-9050-2834

| 민화 | **김미정**

• 서현민화연구소장

• 제24회 성산미술대전 입선
• 제25회 성산미술대전 특선
• 영남미술대전(제15, 16, 17회) 다수 입선
• 2013년 제31회 한국현대미술협회 최우수상
• 2014년 평화문화재단 특선
• 2015년 대한민국 서예문인화대전 특선
• 2015년 제8회 한국민화협회 공모전 특선
• 2016년 서울인사미술대전 우수상

• 2014년 도동시비동산 서현 개인전
• 2015년 3월 30일~4월 5일 아양아트 서현민화회원전
(아름다운 우리 민화)
• 2015년 11월 30일~12월 20일 (사)달구벌나눔문화예술 창립기념전
• 2017년 5월 22일~28일 아양아트 서현민화회원전
• (사)한국민화협회 회원전 5회

• 2015년 4월 서울민화협회 현대민화반 수료
• 2017년 12월 7일 (사)한국민화협회 수료
• 2017년 12월 7일 (사)한국민화협회 민화지도자 자격 수료

• 2015년 3월~현재 (사)한국민화협회 회원

□ 연락처 : 010-2666-4059

| Folk Artist | KIM, Mijeong

- Director of Seohyeon Folk Art Research

- The 24th Seongsan Art Contest winner.
- The 25th Seongsan Art Contest grand prize winner.
- The 15th, 16th, 17th Yeongnam Art Contest winner.
- 2013 - The 31st Korea Modern Art Association grand prize winner.
- 2014 - The Peace & Culture Foundation grand prize winner.
- 2015 - The Korea Calligraphy & Literary Art Contest grand prize winner.
- 2015 - The 8th Korea Folk Art Association Open Contest grand prize winner.
- 2016 - Seoul Insa Art Contest excellence award winner.

- 2014 - Dodong Poem Monument Park Seohyeon private exhibition.
- 2015 - Ayang Art Seohyeon Folk Art Members Exhibition (Our Beautiful Folk Art) from March 30 to April 5.
- 2015 - (Corporation)Dalgubeol Nanoom Culture and Art foundation exhibition from November 30 to December 20.
- 2017 - Ayang Art Seohyeon Folk Art members exhibition from May 22 thru 28.
- (Corporation)Korea Folk Art Association members exhibition(5 times)
- 2015 - April, Seoul Folk Art Association Modern Folk Art Class graduation.
- 2017 - December 7, (Corporation)Korea Folk Art Association graduation.
- 2017 - December 7, (Corporation)Korea Folk Art Association Folk Art Instructor course graduation.

- Since March, 2015-(Corporation)Korea Folk Art Association member.

□ Phone : 010-2666-4059

이 도서의 국립중앙도서관 출판예정도서목록(CIP)은 서지정보유통지원시스템 홈페이지(http://seoji.nl.go.kr)과 국가자료종합목록 구축시스템(http://kolis-net.nl.go.kr)에서 이용하실 수 있습니다.

(CIP제어번호 : CIP2019042145)